The Ultimate OCD Self Help Book

Cure Obsessive Compulsive Disorders Once and For All!

By James L. Shepard

James L Shepard

No part of this book may be reproduced or transmitted in any form whatsoever, electronic, or mechanical, including photocopying, recording, or by any informational storage or retrieval system without express permission from the author.

Copyright © 2014 JNR Publishing Group

All rights reserved.

ISBN-13: 978-1503265950
ISBN-10: 1503265951

CONTENTS

WHAT IS OCD	**5**
SYMPTOMS OF OCD	**8**
CAUSES OF OCD	**10**
OCD AND PERSONAL RELATIONSHIPS	**12**
OCD TREATMENT OPTIONS	**13**
CAN NATURAL PRODUCTS HELP?	**16**
COGNITIVE BEHAVIORAL THERAPY	**17**
SEDONA METHOD	**18**
NEUROTIC FEARS AND DOUBTS MAKE US DEFENSIVE	19
HOW DOES THE SEDONA METHOD WORK?	19
NLP APPROACH TO OCD	**19**
SPINNING TECHNIQUE	**21**
SUBMODALITY MANIPULATION TECHNIQUE	**22**
ANCHORS	**23**

James L Shepard

CONTEXT DEPENDENT **25**

BREAK STATE **26**

MOVIE THEATER THERAPY **26**

OCD PHARMACEUTICAL OPTIONS **27**

OTHER BOOKS BY JNR PUBLISHING GROUP

What is OCD

OCD is a mental health condition that develops a strong sense of unpredictability, doubt, anxiety, or worry in a person's mind and activates habits like constantly re-checking and re-doing stuff you've already done previously. Although sometimes, everyone could feel anxious, afraid, or anxious, these standard emotions and responses assist individuals secure themselves, stay safe, and resolve problems.

These feelings typically do not last long and don't come too often. In the case of individuals with OCD, these feelings are forced to extremes as if the brain does not recognize what's harmful from what's not. There is a constant and remaining stream of fear, doubt, or stress and anxiety in the person's mind, instead of keeping ordinary fear under control. OCD is a kind of stress and anxiety condition identified by persistent, undesirable ideas called obsessions; and recurring behaviors, also called compulsions.

People with OCD are pre-occupied with relentless ideas that bring fear or fret about something that may or may not take place. These adverse thoughts and images are typically hard to get rid of. They have a strong impulse to carry out these routines or recurring habits such as hand cleaning, counting, analyzing, or tidying up stuff with the hopes of avoiding or doing away with neurotic negative ideas.

James L Shepard

The fascinations and compulsions are sometimes associated with each other. A sufferer who frets (obsession) about bacteria and about getting sick might have the impulse or compulsion to clean hands or clean things continuously and consistently.

They are too cautious to touch anything due to fear of bacteria. There are times when the compulsions or the habits don't have anything to do with the compulsions or worry.

As an example, if things on the desk are not arranged suitably, the belief that something bad will happen to a loved one.

The oddity of the habits and worry are so obvious that many individuals try to keep their OCD to themselves. Although medical professionals and scientists still have no idea the real cause of OCD, recent study has actually revealed that OCD is related to levels of an organic chemical in the brain called Serotonin . When the proper flow of Serotonin is obstructed, the brain's "security system" overreacts and misinterprets data. Instead of the brain filtering out these unnecessary ideas, the mind dwells on them and unreasonable fear and doubt is experienced by the sufferer.

Some scientists believe that OCD stems from behavior routines that you learn over time. There is likewise a chance for somebody to develop OCD if he/she has parents or other household members with the disorder although researchers haven't specifically determined it.

OCD conditions can be beaten however specifically what makes it hard for the sufferer is being up against a virtually invisible force in which we discover ourselves in a situation where we find it tough to withstand their demands.

People suffering with OCD do not enjoy the experiences brought on by these intrusive thoughts but are compelled to listen and do the actions accordingly.

There are a lot of different disorders associated with OCD but taking neurotic signs and symptoms and neurotic thoughts are those that work hand in hand together in a comparable way, a damaging force to compete with. Patients with obsessive-compulsive conditions are more vulnerable to anxiety/depression bouts. Distinguishing in between the many variants can be fairly tricky in many cases.

Either way it ruins a sufferer's life, gnawing at their very existence. OCD signifies brain circuitry's bizarre functioning and it includes the Striatum part of the brain. The brain activity patterns of such folks vary from regular people and sufferers with other mental conditions. Researchers have concluded that OCD is in most cases a domestic issue and is a disorder of the brain.

James L Shepard

Streptococcal bacterial infection can develop or worsen the condition of OCD. Adolescents with no family history of OCD can likewise catch it. A lot of teenagers feel embarrassed to discuss their OCDs. They believe that people are going to identify them as crazy and this will cause them to feel insecure and make them feel more ashamed. This also makes it hard for the parents to talk with their youngsters about their OCD conditions, in order to solve them.

Parents have to develop effective communication qualities for this purpose. The Parent's support is additionally essential to the teen patient. His cooperation is extremely crucial along with treatment, due to the fact that if the issue is not treated the teen will grow into a troubled adult.

Symptoms of OCD

A patient suffering from this neurotic condition is aware that his/his compulsions and obsessions are somewhat exaggerated and unreasonable. A person's obsessions and compulsions are understood to trigger distress or problems to one's career and social performance.

The obsessive-compulsive issue is distinguishable in a number of ways. Below are a few of the noteworthy signs and symptoms of this type of dysfunction:

- Extreme worry of contamination. A sufferer diagnosed with OCD is constantly worried about being infected with animal or human body secretions like sweat, vomit, saliva, mucus, feces and pee.

- Incessant aligning or fixing of things or items at their proper or designated placements.

- Habitual obsessions with negative thoughts like chronic fears on particular activities and situations like leaving or eating out of house without bringing the appropriate products.

Some are also afflicted with inappropriate sexual obsessions or ideas.

- Repeated hand cleaning.

- Persistent clearing of throat.

- Endlessly repeating words.

- Gambling dependencies.

- Scratching/ Itching.

- Counting columns and other irrelevant things for hours at a time.

- Eating unsuitable amounts of food.

- Drug dependencies.

James L Shepard

- Checking (light switches, locks, gas cooker is turned off etc.).

- Completing (performing the behavior in specific order again and again, until it is done perfectly. And if interrupted normally he will start all over again).

- Hoarding

Causes of OCD
Medical professionals and researchers still don't quite understand the original cause of OCD; current research has shown that OCD is related to levels of a naturally occurring chemical in the brain called Serotonin. When the appropriate flow of Serotonin is obstructed, the brain's "security" overreacts and misinterprets data. Instead of the brain filtering out these unnecessary thoughts, the mind dwells on them and irrational fear and doubt is experienced by the person.

There is strong proof that OCD can be hereditary. The majority of people with OCD have one or more members of the family having in fact variants of these stress and anxiety disorders, also influenced by the brain's Serotonin production levels.

For this reason, researchers believe that the tendency or predisposition for any sufferer to develop the imbalance that triggers OCD can be received through a person's genes. Having the hereditary tendency does not mean people will absolutely develop OCD right away. It only denotes that chances are higher that they might.

An imbalance of Serotonin levels can also lead to other types of anxiety or depression. Like any other ailment, having OCD is not a person's fault. Fortunately in a vast majority of cases it can be treated with the help from Mental Professionals.

In America approx one in 50 adults presently suffer from the said condition (OCD) double that number for the amount of individuals who in the past that at some point became afflicted by this self damaging disorder.

Any one in general who shows to be at risk to being OCD sufferers are cut off or prevented from carrying out his/his ongoing habits in the home or out on the street is not welcomed with open arms by society.

Children can develop OCD and have neurotic patterns like keeping toys in order. Teenagers likewise can fall under the spell. Parents, if you observe any difference in your kid's behavior then get help right away!

The Amygdala maybe partly to blame

Latest advancement in medical research asserts that the issue lies in the patient's damaged Amygdala, the human brain's center for typical feelings and emotions. The

James L Shepard

Amygdala of the person suffering with OCD is thought to be acting up.

OCD and Personal Relationships

The question now is what if this person is your partner, spouse, boyfriend or husband? This somewhat odd behavior undoubtedly sets the phase for strains in a relationship. Is it worth it? Can OCD and relationships really work?

Like the Amygdala itself, the relationship of a non-sufferer with a person dealing with OCD, is constantly on the verge of misfiring. The non-sufferer feels incessantly uneasy or awkward trying to comprehend the peculiar habits of the partner. The OCD sufferer could feel an excellent degree of desperation, knowing that their loved ones truly have a tough time relating with them. From this perspective, both the OCD and non-OCD folks suffer all the same.

Multiply a singular event of this friction between those involved for several months, even years and you'll get a pretty good idea what they have to deal with. The pressure is tremendous, with both the parties involved.

Looked at from a different point of view, living with person suffering with OCD can be a blessing. A stable relationship with an OCD may be an opportunity to reflect on the important things that we truly treasure about these people. This relationship, will very much not only challenge our traditional concept of loving relationships, but will absolutely challenge us to understand the definition of a fully committed relationship.

OCD Treatment Options

Typically, OCD is treated with 3 kinds of anxiety treatment options:

Cognitive treatment, behavioral therapy and even medications. As for the cognitive and behavior modifications, among the list of recommended treatments advised to OCD victims is direct exposure and negative response prohibition.

Recent researches show that a good number of OCD patients fail to look for clinical aid due to stigma or shame of having any type of anxiety disorder.

Another observed reason for unaccounted for OCD condition is that some individuals are not aware that they even have this serious neurotic disorder.

Obsessive Compulsive Disorder in the past was thought of as being untreatable. However medical professionals in today's world refused to be beaten and continued to investigate day and night searching for answers behind why a patient believed their OCD signified insanity- that

James L Shepard

their actions sent out signals of mental instability. In other words are they really crazy as they thought?

Fortunately the answer is no. Treatment is easily available combined with friends and family who care and dedication to help. This ailment or condition can be quashed!

To get control of our behaviors first we have to face up to the OCD and believe in ourselves that we can fight this battle single handed if need be. I say single handed simply because this fight is one sided (between you and yourself).

Medication is readily offered to combat and alleviate the signs and symptoms however for better outcomes you need to work hand in hand with prescribed medications and listen to clinical advisors. This approach has proven to be successful for many sufferers of OCD. Patients in desperation, who decided enough is enough!, go on to topple this illness once and for all, and winning their freedoms back!

The cure is out there whether you decide to take it or not is another matter. Independence beats being a prisoner within your own thoughts where mind over matter, matters. All patients differ where sometimes symptoms are more serious than that of others.

There is no need to attempt and beat this alone, yes I did discuss this was between you and yourself, but where is the harm in having a little support behind you, right?

With medication, behavioral therapy, and counseling, patients with OCD can truly start to lead rather normal lives once more. Talking to your physician about your OCD issues is the very first step to regulating your quality of life and health. This condition can be devastating, but with a little hard work, one can get rid of OCD guaranteed!

To be identified with OCD, one needs to fulfill requirements stated by the Diagnostic and Statistical Manual of Mental Disorders (DSM-IV). For a client to take advantage of treatment, they must realize that the compulsions are unreasonable and excessive.

Possession of the above discussed signs or symptoms are not always an absolute medical diagnosis. Treatment typically includes behavioral or cognitive treatment, medications or a mix of the three. Psychiatric therapy mixed with psychotropic medications like selective Serotonin reuptake inhibitors or SSRIs have shown to be more reliable than either option alone.

Continued research is discovering brand-new and enhanced treatments all the time to assist people with OCD to lead productive satisfying lives.

James L Shepard

Can Natural Products Help?

There are a number of amazing natural herbs that have actually been shown to work with mental issues, such as St. John's Wort. This is a herb that has actually been scientifically shown to assist with depression and when used by someone with OCD, it can also support to minimize a few of their symptoms.

Another aspect of OCD that is typically not treated is the underlying worry or stress that a person is going through. For those issues, other herbs can assist to produce a more peaceful mind and body, where the problems of OCD won't always grow. You may visit curezone.org, join the free forum and find out the overwhelming number of natural health options available to you.

What Other Treatments Are There? In addition to these natural treatments that typically come in the form of dietary supplements you will likewise discover that natural medicine such as hypnosis, acupuncture, and others can assist to reduce tension and pressure in a person's life, which frequently coincide with issues associated with OCD.

There are also some new and ingenious option treatments that involve particular therapies that are used to improve a person's confidence, how they feel about themselves and their life, and deal with a few of the fears that they have. These treatments can help to improve a sufferer's total outlook, which in turn can turn their focus far from their habitual or ritual behaviors that are getting in the way of them living their life.

Cognitive Behavioral Therapy
Cognitive behavior modification is an action-oriented type of psychosocial therapy that presumes that maladaptive, or faulty, thinking patterns cause maladaptive habits and "negative" feelings. The treatment concentrates on changing a sufferer's thoughts in order to change his/his habits and psychological well-being. This is typically a long, pricey and agonizing procedure.

Providing CBT for obsessive-compulsive disorder (OCD) needs an in-depth understanding of the phenomenology and the mechanics by which specific cognitive procedures and behaviors keep the symptoms of the disorder. A cognitive-behavioral design of OCD begins with the observation that intrusive thoughts, doubts or images are nearly universal in the general population and their content is identical to everyone. The difference in between a normal invasive thought and an obsessional thought lies both in the significance that individuals with OCD connect to the event or content of the intrusions and in their response to the thought or image.

James L Shepard

OCD is the application of cognitive management to assist the client to develop a therapeutically sound response-set to this stress and anxiety affliction. Cognitive conceptualization concentrates on eliminating the sense of guilt, shame which can be pervasive among OCD clients.

Conceiving the treatment and comprehending the dynamics of OCD permit for a greater sense of dedication to taking part in the difficult treatment recommendations.

It is vital to note that one's believed content and one's authentic beliefs can be extremely different. People are exempt for the ideas that strike them through automatic cognitive processes. Helping people to separate themselves from the emotional and/or moral implications of what this condition seems to represent, is a significant part of cognitive conceptualization.

Sedona Method
Sedona Method is an easy-to-learn, do-it-yourself system designed to reveal to you the best ways to tap your natural ability to let go of any unwanted feeling, and all forms of obsessive/neurotic habits.

It can be used in life to obtain instant relief of any symptoms. The Sedona Method also helps to quickly break the patterns of thought and behavior that trigger these sensations to prevent recurring.

Neurotic fears and doubts make us defensive
When we are defensive, we are holding in mind specifically what we do not desire, and so that's specifically what we get. As you release your defensiveness, you see options instead of problems and limitations. As you naturally hold in mind what you desire, you'll understand ways to be pro-active and succeed whenever.

How does the Sedona Method work?
As you use the Method, you will discover gradually that situations and experiences that you used to find most tiring or troubling will end up being minimized and soon you might even forget that you used to have those type of negative experiences.

OCD is defined primarily by a very "noisy" mind. The Sedona Method neutralizes this, and allows the suffering person to regain control over his mind. It might not work in all cases of OCD however.

NLP Approach to OCD
In NLP we identify how the person does the mental process of OCD, that is specifically what is the mental procedure, the thoughts that are applied to develop the behavior? In general the OCD person will basically make images in their mind, talk to themselves and produce a

feeling. By working with the sensory modalities i.e. manipulating the self talk, the vividness or blurriness of mental pictures, what emotions and sensations are felt etc, the mental process can be changed such that it no longer produces the old behavior as strongly.

The effect we want is to bring awareness to the actions such that they end up being intentional, decisive and purposeful. To gain total control of your internal thoughts, mental imagery and self talk! To develop a sense of congruence within yourself that you know with both mind and heart that the behavior and your internal mental processes are what you want to be there- deliberately- by design!

Treatment includes breaking the OCD mental pattern (every patient has a unique, customized OCD pattern, developed from his own unique beliefs, values and life experiences). Treatment is not so much a concern of putting the patient into a hypnotic trance to treat him; rather it is a question of smashing the hypnotic trance- OCD he is already in.

You see, when somebody is so preoccupied by stress, anxiety and fear that he is unknowingly developing rituals which he repetitively carries out in an attempt to diminish those intense feelings. For example if he's unreasonably scared of germs, sickness etc, that fear causes that hand washing compulsion (as Michael Jackson also suffered from).

He is making big pictures in his mind accompanied by strong feelings, and his attention is so concentrated on those things that he is in a modified- OCD robotic- trance state.

So perhaps that very first thing to do with that treatment procedure is get that patient into a more relaxed state and endeavor to reframe that situation. We are all creatures of habit and a lot of that time our routines serve us well, however if you need OCD treatment it probably means your routines have actually gotten just a bit out of control.

Spinning Technique
- Stop, take yourself to a quiet place and concentrate on the cause of it. When you begin to think about it carefully, two things are likely to happen: (1) you can expect to see a picture or images in your mind; (2) you can expect to arrive at a nervous feeling someplace. Now, replay that image in your mind and, as you do so, notice which way that feeling is moving in your body.

- Play that entire sequence of images in your mind and as you are carrying this out, spin that feeling in the opposite direction.

- Notice as you do this how the feelings actually change.

James L Shepard

- Now play that sequence of pictures again and this time spin the feeling even quicker in that opposite direction this time and see the difference in your feelings. It feels weird doesn't it? The exact process or experience of fear becomes unrecognizable when inverted! Any feeling can be destroyed this way.

Repeat the exercise for a total amount of at least five times and repeat as necessary.

Each time you spin that feeling in the opposite direction, make it quicker and stronger until you arrive at that moment when that anxiety doesn't seem to matter anymore. After this OCD treatment you now have the tools to control your feelings and feel much better.

Submodality Manipulation Technique
In any internal experience, there will often be a picture, feeling, audio etc. Keep in mind where that picture is in your mind's eye. Is it directly in front of you? To one side or the other? Up or down? Are you outside that picture or are you seeing that image through your very own eyes? Is that image a movie or is it a still? Is it 2 or 3-dimensional? What are that sounds connected to that image? Are they loud or soft? Exactly what is their pitch and speed? Are they clear or remote/muffled? Keep in

mind that feelings connected with that picture? Where are they? Which direction are they moving? Etc.

Attempt to alter that image. If it is small, make it bigger. Make that color vibrant. This is called modifying the sub modality, and by playing with the sub modalities of the experience, you gain masterful control over that experience!

Anchors
Anchors are a few of that most effective tools in NLP; they are very reliable at OCD treatment. Essentially what you want to do is capture the moments you felt extremely happy, confident, fearless and other positive emotions that you like which happens to be the direct opposite of the bad feelings you experience from OCD. Do remember to also play with Sub modalities, and the general rule is if you can make the sounds/pictures/smells/feelings bigger/louder/stronger etc in some way, the stronger those internal experiences will be. Doing the exact opposite will reduce the experience, which is useful for bad or negative thoughts and feelings we want to get rid of.

With that said, all you need to do is associate a particular sound, image or body sensation to both the desired states and negative states. Phobias are actually examples of naturally occurring programmed anchors that bring about

James L Shepard

states of fears and anxieties triggered by the anchor like a spider, centipede, heights etc.

Most just recommend capturing the positive states. However by also anchoring the negative states? You gain power over them!

For example you can Anchor to your left pinky (by pinching on it, when you playback that state) of wanting to wash your hands cause of fear of contamination or diseases. Repeat this process several times to make sure you set the anchor properly. Remember to put a state interrupt in between anchoring setups by putting your mind somewhere else random, and then proceed with your Anchoring setup/programming.

Assuming you have anchored your left pinky with fear of diseases? All you need to do is press on your Pinky, and all those bad feelings come rushing in. You can then proceed to destroy or alter it!

Perhaps while having sex, or while watching a comedy show, or eating the most amazing dish, you can press on it, notice how that feeling of fear of diseases gets tainted.

Note: You need to set a real strong anchor, and make sure the states you will use to alter the problematic states are STRONGER; otherwise you'll anchor the fear or bad states to the pleasurable states.

You'll feel paranoid of getting a disease when you have sex, watch comedy shows, or eat at a fine dining restaurant. Lol.

As you are now familiar with this exercise, you can practice making yourself feel delighted for no specific reason, at any time you choose. If you continuously make a practice of feeling these positive states and firing off that anchor, you can expect to develop a new habit to replace the old anxiety.

Context Dependent

OCD might become a regular part of your life while you are inside your house or in some other context or environment where you may be able to manage yourself more easily than when you are in public for example. Why? You may simply find it awkward to give in to your compulsions when you are around other people. That shows that you know how to have control, you just don't want to.

Exploit these opportunities! Invite good friends into your house often. When your house becomes, basically, a public location, you'll be less lured to give in to your obsessions and compulsions, and over time your brain will be immediately set to perceive your home as someplace where these activities are not ok. Notice how Anchoring principles are also working in that setting.

James L Shepard

Break State
The more a sufferer tries to deny that OCD thought or focus on that fear, the stronger that thought ends up being. The next time you experience a compulsive thought, get into the practice of never dwelling on it at all. When that unfavorable thought comes, STOP IT! Stop focusing on that thought and to think of something else pronto!

Movie theater Therapy
One approach utilized to resolve OCD is called Cinema Therapy, a treatment method that utilizes films with characters and stories that are somewhat comparable to that specific situation dealt with by the particular patient.

Throughout the session, the client is often asked to keep in mind the plot, characters, situations, and other considerable images in that movie. The client is encouraged to verbalize his comments and insights into the film.

The objective of Cinema Therapy is to teach the patient ways to see his life and current problems in a detached, objective and analogous fashion in relation to the movie. Detachment permits an individual to think objectively and arrive at certain commitments or action strategies to prevent obsessive-compulsive habits.

Relating your life to films or other works of fiction can be an excellent therapy due to the fact that it works as a mirror of who we are. A metaphor of the real and the surreal. By seeing other people on the silver screen exhibit the same failures and challenges, the patient becomes comfortable in acknowledging that he too is human-- and that realization becomes that major step to real recovery.

OCD Pharmaceutical Options

People struggling with OCD have traditionally looked for anxiety relief by means of antidepressants and similar drugs. These medications help make Serotonin more conveniently available in some parts of the brain. Serotonin is a compound inside the brain that assists and manage anger, hostilities, mood swings, anxiety, as well as libido and cravings for food.

Fluoxetine, typically offered under the brand name Prozac, has become quite possibly the most prescribed medication for OCD patients. For some clients, drugs are required as a consequence of the severity of their conditions.

Some with OCD can receive effective treatments that consists of Psychotherapy and consumption of prescription drugs like:

James L Shepard

- Fluoxetine

- Fluvoxamine

- Clomipramine

- Paroxetine

- Sertraline

and other Serotonin reuptake inhibitors.

If you liked this book, please consider leaving a positive review so that others may gain the same insights and knowledge that could also help them!

I do not have an advertising budget, so support in the form of positive word of mouth from people like you would be immensely appreciated!

Thank you for buying this book and till the next time!

James L Shepard

This guide is not intended as and may not be construed as an alternative to or a substitute for professional business, mental counseling, therapy or medical services and advice.

The authors, publishers, and distributors of this guide have made every effort to ensure the validity, accuracy, and timely nature of the information presented here. However, no guarantee is made, neither direct nor implied, that the information in this guide or the techniques described herein are suitable for or applicable to any given individual person or group of persons, nor that any specific result will be achieved. The authors, publishers, and distributors of this guide will be held harmless and without fault in all situations and causes arising from the use of this information by any person, with or without professional medical supervision. The information contained in this book is for informational and entertainment purposes only. It not intended as a professional advice or a recommendation to act.

No part of this book may be reproduced or transmitted in any form whatsoever, electronic, or mechanical, including photocopying, recording, or by any informational storage or retrieval system without express permission from the author.

© Copyright 2014, JNR Publishing

Date of publication Dec 23, 2014

All rights reserved.

Other books by JNR Publishing Group

The Seduction Force Multiplier 1- Bring Out Your FULL Seduction powers through the Power of Routines, Drills, Scripting and Protocols

The Seduction Force Multiplier 2 - Scripts and Routines Book

James L Shepard

The Seduction Force Multiplier 3- PUA Routines Memory Transplant Package

The Seduction Force Multiplier 4 - Situational PUA Scripts and Routines

The Seduction Force Multiplier V - Target Auto Response Package

The Seduction Force Multiplier VI - PUA Innergame, Mindsets and Attitudes

James L Shepard

[Shielded Heart - How To Stop Yourself From Falling For A Seduction Target](#)

[How To Cheat Proof Your Relationships](#)

[Secrets to Hacking Your Brain- Be Your Own Therapist](#)

Hypno Machines - How To Convert Every Object In Your Environment As a Device For Psychological and Emotional Manipulator

The Art Of Virtual Practice 2 - Learning and Mastery Of Any Skill At Lighting Speeds!

James L Shepard

How to Operate with Your Full Potential and Talents

How To Master Resilience And Be Invincible To Life's Disappointments And Failures

The X-Factor Manual - **Learn How To be A Model Even If You Don't Look Like One**

The Age Erase System - Hypnotic Anti Aging Serum

Develop Insane Self Confidence and Naturally Unleash The Supermodel Within

James L Shepard

The Persuaders Guide To Eliminating Resistance And Getting Compliance

The Art of Invisible Compliance - How To Make People Do What You Want Effortlessly

Unstoppable and Fearless - Know What You Want and Get It

Just Go- Having The Courage and Will to Pursue Your Dreams

How To Make Better Life Decisions

James L Shepard

How To Diet Like a Machine- Make Any Diet Program Work With Ease

Friends into Lovers: Escape and Never be Trapped In The Friendzone Ever Again!

The Permanent Anti-jealousy Solution

The TEN Game Operations Manual: How To Get Extremely Gorgeous 10s Consistently and Predictably!

How Not To Give a Shit!: The Art of Not Caring

James L Shepard

Perfecting Your Game: How To Reach Mastery Through Perfection Of Game!

Manipulative Eye Contact Techniques: Install thoughts and feelings just with your eyes!

The Injector Protocol: How To Inject Your Essence Literally Into Everything!

Hyper Learning Techniques: How To Learn at Super Speeds!

The Anti-AA Eradication System : **100% Foolproof Approach Anxiety Elimination Techniques and Protocols To Enable You To Start Approaching Dozens of Women Today!**

James L Shepard

The Ultimate Dog Training Crash Course

Maximized Energy = Maximized Potential: How to pursue the most difficult tasks with your maximum energies and potential!

!

Tough Love: Surviving and Winning The Most Difficult Romance Games, Relationships and Lovers From Hell!

Acting and Comedy Techniques for Seducers and PUAs

Putting Mind Control In Your Daily Life

James L Shepard

Seducing the UNseduceable Man: Specialized seduction techniques for the impossible to get man!

Be A Human Lie Detector: Detect High-Level, Covert Communications of Persuaders, Seducers and Other Manipulators!

2- Styles of Communications:Perfectly calibrated communications everytime!

Techniques on Developing Irresistible Charisma at Work: A tactical-manual on how to be the ultimate People-person everyone likes and follows!

James L Shepard

The Ultimate Guide On Manufacturing REAL Luck

Proven Strategies To Taking Control Of Your Life By Creating Your Own Luck!

Imitate, Innovate and Annihilate! How to Clone And Improve On competitors' Best Products and Services Effectively!

How To Increase Reputation and Popularity! Applying Practical Brand Management Principles For Businesses and Individuals

The Ultimate Business Competition Guide: Reverse Engineer The competition and Make 'em eat your dust!

James L Shepard

How to Achieve Mental Mastery by Maximizing Your Brain Performance!

Reach Your Full Brain Potential by Adopting Proven Thinking Methods to Drastically improve Your Mental Skills, Discipline and Development

Develop Irresistible Skills of Persuasion, Motivation and Leadership at Work And With Friends!

Learn the fine art and science of persuasion and motivation to effectively influence people...

[The Ultimate Guide On How to Be Naturally Persuasive](#)

Influence People Without Manipulative Persuasion Tactics and Strategies

[Develop Powerful Business Thinking and Reasoning Processes](#)

James L Shepard

How to choose the PERFECT thinking styles to think smarter,better,clearer for any situation!

The Ultimate Guide to Developing a High Performance Mentality

How to achieve anything you want by thinking like an Overachiever!

The Ultimate Guide to Counselling, Coaching and Mentoring

The Handbook of Coaching Skills and Tools to Improve Results and Performance Of your Team!

The Ultimate Guide on Developing Conflict Resolution Techniques for Workplace Conflicts

How to develop workplace positivity, morale, communications.

James L Shepard

The Ultimate Guide on Proven Communication Techniques and Presentation Secrets **How to Communicate with Power and Improve Your Persuasion IQ at Work and in Everyday Life!**

The Corporate Warriors Manual

Applying Military Principles to Conquer Business and Life!

The Ultimate Burnout Cure

Re-ignite your passions in life and work!

The Winner's Code

How to unleash the winner within

Maximizing Results Through Minimalism

Get the most out of life by focusing only on the essentials!

The Ultimate Guide To Executing Strategies, Plans & Tactics

Practicing the Art of Execution

The Ultimate Collaboration & Synergy Guide

How to bring out the best performance and results from everyone!

Being the Action-Man in Business

How to start making things happen today!

Hit the Ground Running in Business

Learn Must-know Business Fundamentals for the New Entrepreneur

Conflicting Views

Tactfully handle any conflicts in any organization

The Ultimate Guide on Developing Patience

Be a better leader by expanding your patience!

Designing & Projecting Powerful First Impressions

Pragmatic Time Management Techniques

Getting things done on time, everytime!

The Fine Art of Decision Making

Make things happen by making the right calls!

The Ultimate Guide to Building & Managing the Perfect Team

Parenting and Disciplining Strong-Willed Children

Advanced parenting techniques for defiant children!

Advanced Parenting Techniques of Rebellious Teens

The ultimate guide to parenting difficult teens from hell!

The E.Q. Genius

Mastering Emotional Intelligence

The Ultimate Guide to the Placebo Effect

Understanding and exploiting Placebo effects in health & life!

Mastering Creativity and Inspiration

James L Shepard

Cures to your Creativity Problems Revealed!

The Ultimate Guide to Developing Belief in Yourself

The Inner and Outer Games of Developing Trust and Belief in your Capabilities!

Dealing With Horrible Bosses

How To Handle Bad Managers at Work

Just in your head

How to eliminate panic and anxiety disorders

How to handle tough situations

Finding Inner Strength to survive the toughest crisis and life challenges

Using the Laws Of Attraction in Sex, Love, Dating & Relationships

Exploit LOA to get what you want!

Why So Insecure?

How To Overcome Emotional Insecurities Dead In It's Tracks!

The Ultimate OCD Self Help Book

Cure Obsessive Compulsive Disorders Once and For All!

The Art of Risk Management

Learn to Manage Risks Like a Pro

You Are Your Own Worst Enemy

How To Stop Self Sabotaging Behaviors Once and For All!

Make Your Own Affirmations, Autosuggestions and Self Hypnosis Products

Drastically Improve ANY Aspect of Your Life On Autopilot!

Taming the Beasts

The Ultimate Guide How To Handle Difficult People

Healthy Sweet Tooth

50 quick and easy mouth-watering healthy desserts to satisfy your cravings

Hypnotic Banter Techniques:

Using Humor For Hypnotic Persuasions in Seduction & Business

James L Shepard

Books Available Soon

The Pet Whisperer

Teach Yourself To Communicate With Your Beloved Pets & Animals

The Mind of Swindlers, Con Men, Fraudsters & Scam Artists

Learn to Scam-proof your life!

My Buddy is `FEAR'

Using your own fear to get things done!

The Seducer's Guide To Developing A Good Sense Of Humor

Be Sexy & Funny, Without Being a Dancing Monkey!

How to Fail Your Way to Success

Use Failures to Weed Out the Duds

Layman's Guide to NLP Modelling

How to be anything you want to be!

The Child Whisperer

Persuasion Techniques to make children want or hate anything you want